Divine Healing

This Prayer Journal Belongs to:

Copyright © 2023 by Let Your Light Shine Press

Be Still and Know

Psalm 46:10

As a special thanks for your purchase
Download your FREE Gift:
http://go.azizituere.com/healinggift

Please leave a Amazon review at
http://go.azizituere.com/healingreview

Have you seen our other great offerings?

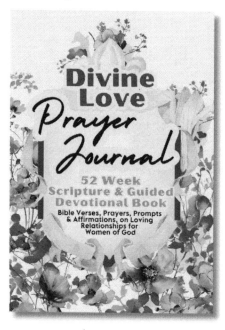

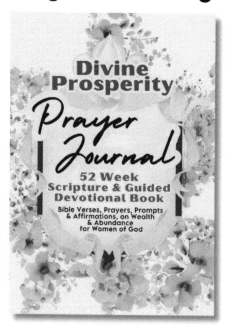

She reached out and
touched his cloak, and
immediately her bleeding
stopped. Jesus said to her,
"Daughter, your faith has
healed you."

In the Bible, we see many stories of women who were healed by their faith in God. The power of prayer has been recognized for thousands of years as a way to connect with a higher power and bring about positive change in our lives.

In the pages of this journal, you will find weekly guided prompts to help you pray for physical, emotional, and spiritual healing. Each entry will include a Bible verse, a prayer statement, a positive affirmation, and a guided journal prompt to help you stay focused on your healing journey. We encourage you to use this journal as a dedicated practice, carving out time each day to reflect, pray, and write.

Approach this journal with an open heart and mind, allowing infinite intelligence to guide you towards healing and health. Through this practice, we hope that you will find the healing, strength, comfort, and peace that comes from a deep and abiding relationship with the infinite intelligence that flows to you, through you, and all around you.

We are grateful and overjoyed that you chose us to support you alongside your healing journey.

We want to assure you that this journal is not intended to replace professional health advice or treatment. We encourage you to seek out professionals according to your own personal needs.

May God bless you and guide you on your path towards wellness.

Table of Contents

How to use
Divine Healing

01 Set aside a specific time and space. Find a quiet and comfy place to focus and let your thoughts flow freely.

02 Close your eyes and begin by taking a few deep relaxing breaths. Imagine the ever-present healing power flowing through you now. Feel its presence and warm glow.

03 Next, read the scripture of the week and accompanying message. Allow yourself to settle into a reflective state to receive the deeper meaning of the passage.

04 Then write down your thoughts and reflections. Be honest and open, and try not to judge yourself or your writing.

05 If you start to feel overwhelmed or distracted, take a break to stretch, or do something else that helps you refocus.

06 Read over what you have written. Look for patterns, insights, or areas for growth. Use this self-reflection to identify specific actions you can take to move forward.

07 End reading the affirmation and prayer, it reinforces insights and growth gained through your devotional journaling practice. Repeat throughout the week, as needed.

Contemplation

3 John 1:2

Beloved, I pray that all may go well with you and that you may be in good health, as it goes well with your soul. [ESV]

Unity of Being

Our bodies and souls are connected and have a powerful influence on one another. When we take care of our bodies, we are also taking care of our souls, and vice versa. So it's important to prioritize our health and well-being in all aspects of our lives.

How can you better prioritize your health in your daily life? What small changes can you make to take care of your body and soul?

_____

....

_____

....

_____

....

_____

....

Prayer Request   **Prayer Granted**

AFFIRMATION

I am committed to prioritizing my health and well-being, knowing that it benefits both my body and soul.

PRAYER

Dear God, please guide me to make choices that support my health and well-being. Help me to honor the connection between my body and soul.

Contemplation

Psalm 23:3

He restores my soul. He leads me in paths of righteousness for his name's sake. [ESV]

Restored for Glory

We tend to think we should keep going until everything is finished, but life goes on until the end. Being "done" can be an illusion. Rest is essential for physical and mental well-being, allowing us to heal and recharge. Moreover, resting demonstrates our trust in God's constant provision, which eliminates the need for unnecessary stress.

Are there any areas of your life where you need to prioritize rest and self-care? How can you make time for rest in your daily routine?

_____

....

_____

....

_____

....

_____

Prayer Request   **Prayer Granted**

AFFIRMATION

I honor my need for rest and self-care, and prioritize my health and well-being.

PRAYER

Dear God, help me to prioritize rest and self-care in my life. Guide me towards activities and practices that will promote healing and well-being.

Contemplation

Psalm 103:2-3

Praise the Lord, my soul, and forget not all His benefits—who forgives all your sins and heals all your diseases. [ESV]

Soul's Grateful Praise

Sometimes in times of sickness or struggle, it can be easy to lose sight of all the ways that God has already blessed us. By taking time to remember His benefits, we can gain a greater sense of hope and healing.

What are some of the benefits that God has already provided in your life, and how can you cultivate gratitude for them in the midst of illness?

_____

....

_____

....

_____

....

_____

Prayer Request   **Prayer Granted**

....

....

....

....

AFFIRMATION
I am grateful for all of God's blessings and trust in His healing power.

PRAYER
Dear God, thank you for your forgiveness and healing power. Help me to remember all your benefits and to trust in your goodness for my health.

Contemplation

Isaiah 53:5

But He was pierced for our transgressions, he was crushed for our iniquities; the punishment that brought us peace was on Him, and by His wounds we are healed.

Redemption Brings Restoration

In times of pain and strife, remember the One who gave His life. By His wounds, we find healing and peace, redeemed and restored by His grace without cease.

How can you bring the power of Christ's wounds into your own healing journey? What can you do to deepen your faith in His healing power?

_____

....

_____

....

_____

....

Prayer Request   **Prayer Granted**

AFFIRMATION
By Christ's wounds, I am healed and made whole.

PRAYER
Dear Jesus, thank you for bearing our pain and suffering on the cross.
Help me to trust in the power of your wounds for my healing.

Contemplation

James 5:15

And the prayer offered in faith will make the sick person well; the Lord will raise them up. If they have sinned, they will be forgiven.

Faith That Heals

Prayer offered in faith has the power to heal us from our physical and emotional afflictions. By cultivating a deep and abiding faith in God's healing power, we can open ourselves to the possibility of miraculous healing.

How can you deepen your faith in God's healing power? What are some steps you can take to cultivate a deeper sense of trust and surrender?

_____

....

_____

_____

....

_____

Prayer Request   **Prayer Granted**

AFFIRMATION
I have faith in God's healing power and trust in His plan for my life.

PRAYER
Dear God, I offer my prayers in faith, trusting in your healing power.
Help me to deepen my faith and to surrender to your will for my life.

Contemplation

1 Peter 5:7

Cast all your anxiety on Him because He cares for you.

Surrendered Strength

Surrendering control is hard, but God can heal and mend the scars. Give Him your worries, let Him restore, His love and grace will heal you to the core.

What worries and anxieties are weighing you down? How can you surrender them to God and trust in His care for you?

_____

....

_____

....

_____

....

_____

Prayer Request	Prayer Granted
....	....
....	....
....	....
....	

AFFIRMATION
I trust in God's care and surrender all my worries to Him for healing.

PRAYER
Dear God, I surrender all my worries and anxieties to you. Help me to trust in your care and to release all that is holding me back from healing.

Contemplation

Psalm 139:14

I praise you because I am fearfully and wonderfully made; your works are wonderful, I know that full well.

God's Masterpiece in Me

Your health journey is unique and there is no one-size-fits-all solution. Embrace your individuality and focus on your progress rather than comparing yourself to others. Remember that your body is a gift from God and deserves to be treated with care and respect.

What small changes can you make to prioritize your health and care for your body? How can you celebrate your unique health journey?

_____

....

_____

....

_____

....

_____

Prayer Request   **Prayer Granted**

AFFIRMATION
I embrace my unique health journey and trust in God's plan for my wellbeing.

PRAYER
Dear God, thank you for creating me fearfully and wonderfully. Help me to prioritize my health and honor the gift of my body.

Contemplation

Proverbs 17:22

A cheerful heart is good medicine, but a crushed spirit dries up the bones.

Medicine of Cheer

Joy is a powerful force in our health journey. When we cultivate a cheerful heart, we invite good medicine into our lives. Focus on the things that bring you joy and let them fill your heart with healing and vitality.

What brings you joy? How can you incorporate more joy into your health journey?

_____

....

_____

....

_____

....

Prayer Request   **Prayer Granted**

AFFIRMATION
I invite the healing power of joy into my health journey.

PRAYER
Dear God, I ask for a cheerful heart and the healing power of joy. Help me to focus on the things that bring me joy and cultivate a heart of gratitude.

Contemplation

Isaiah 58:8

Then your light will break forth like the dawn, and your healing will quickly appear; then your righteousness will go before you, and the glory of the Lord will be your rear guard.

Healing Breaks Dawn

Do you long for a life filled with light and hope, yet feel lost in the darkness of despair? Let God's healing power restore your heart, shining light into the deepest parts. With His glory as your guard, look forward with hope to the blessings that are yet to come.

How can you open yourself up to God's healing light? In what areas of your life do you need the light to shine more brightly?

_____

....

_____

....

_____

....

_____

Prayer Request   **Prayer Granted**

....

....

....

....

AFFIRMATION
I trust in the light of God to bring healing and restoration to my whole being.

PRAYER
God, I seek your light and guidance for my healing and restoration. Help me to walk in righteousness and trust in your power to heal.

Contemplation

Psalm 107:20

He sent out His word and healed them, and delivered them from their destruction. [ESV]

God's Healing Word

God's word has the power to heal and deliver us from all afflictions. But we must believe in His promises and declare them over our lives to activate their power.

In what ways can you incorporate God's healing promises into your daily life? What words of healing can you speak over yourself today?

_____

. . . .

_____

. . . .

_____

. . . .

_____

Prayer Request   **Prayer Granted**

AFFIRMATION
I believe in the power of God's word to heal and deliver me from all afflictions.

PRAYER
Dear God, I thank you for the healing power of your word. Help me to declare your promises of healing over my life every day.

Contemplation

Jeremiah 30:17

But I will restore you to health and heal your wounds, declares the Lord.

Wholeness Through Grace

No matter the depths of your pain and suffering, God promises to restore your health and well-being. Through His infinite grace and love, your wounds will be healed and your scars revealed.

**In what areas of your life do you need healing and restoration?
How can you trust in God's promise to bring wholeness to
your body, mind, and spirit?**

_____

....

_____

....

_____

....

Prayer Request   **Prayer Granted**

AFFIRMATION

I trust in God's promise to restore me to health and wholeness. His love and care will bring healing to every part of my life.

PRAYER

Dear God, thank you for the promise of restoration and healing. I trust in Your love and care to bring me back to health and wholeness.

Contemplation

Psalm 91:10-11

No harm will overtake you, no disaster will come near your tent. For He will command his angels concerning you to guard you in all your ways.

Divine Angelic Protection

God sends His angels to watch over us and protect us from harm. By trusting in His love and care, we can feel safe and secure in all situations.

In what areas of your life do you need protection and safety? How can you trust in God's angels to watch over you and keep you from harm?

_____

....

_____

....

_____

....

_____

Prayer Request   **Prayer Granted**

AFFIRMATION
I am protected and watched over by God's angels. His love and care keep me safe in all situations.

PRAYER
Dear God, thank you for sending your angels to protect and watch over me. I trust in your love and care to keep me safe and secure.

Contemplation

Proverbs 4:20-22

My son, pay attention to what I say; turn your ear to my words. Do not let them out of your sight, keep them within your heart; for they are life to those who find them and health to one's whole body.

Listening for Life

God's word is a powerful tool for healing our bodies and minds. By keeping His words in our hearts and minds, we can experience His healing power in all areas of our lives.

In what ways can you make God's word a regular part of your day-to-day life? How can you use it to promote your physical and mental health?

_____

....

_____

....

_____

....

_____

Prayer Request   **Prayer Granted**

AFFIRMATION

God's word is a source of life and health for me. I will make a daily habit of incorporating His words into my life to promote healing.

PRAYER

Dear God, help me to keep Your words close to my heart and mind, so that I may experience the healing power of Your love and wisdom in my life.

Contemplation

Psalm 147:3

He heals the brokenhearted and binds up their wounds.

Divine Healing Comfort

Emotional pain can manifest in physical symptoms, and it's important to address our emotional needs as part of our overall health. God is our ultimate healer and promises to bind up our wounds. It's important to allow ourselves to feel our emotions and seek support when we need it.

In what areas of your life do you need emotional healing? How can you open yourself up to God's healing power?

_____

....

_____

....

_____

....

Prayer Request   **Prayer Granted**

AFFIRMATION
God is my healer and I am open to receiving His emotional and physical healing.

PRAYER
Dear God, thank you for your healing power. I surrender my emotional pain to you and trust in your loving care.

Contemplation

Matthew 8:17

He took up our infirmities and bore our diseases.

Faith in His Power

Jesus took on our pain and sickness, and through Him, we can find healing. But it's important to believe in His power to heal us and have faith that He will restore us to health.

How can you strengthen your faith in Christ's healing power? What steps can you take to trust in His ability to restore you to health?

_____

....

_____

....

_____

....

_____

Prayer Request   **Prayer Granted**

....

....

....

....

AFFIRMATION
Through Christ, I am healed and whole.

PRAYER
Dear Jesus, I believe in Your healing power and ask for Your touch in my life. Help me to trust in Your ability to restore me to health.

Contemplation

1 Corinthians 6:19-20

Do you not know that your bodies are temples of the Holy Spirit, who is in you, whom you have received from God? You are not your own; you were bought at a price. Therefore honor God with your bodies.

Honoring Our Bodies

Our bodies are a gift from God and we are called to treat them with respect and care. By taking care of our bodies through exercise, healthy eating, and self-care, we are honoring God's gift to us.

How can you honor God with your body? What changes can you make to treat your body with more respect and care?

_____

....

_____

....

_____

....

_____

Prayer Request   **Prayer Granted**

....

....

....

....

AFFIRMATION
My body is a temple of the Holy Spirit, and I choose to honor God
by taking care of it.

PRAYER
*Dear God, help me to honor you by taking care of my body. Guide me
to make choices that nourish and strengthen me.*

Contemplation

Psalm 91:16

With long life I will satisfy Him and show Him my salvation.

Eternal Life Promise

God desires for us to live long and healthy lives, and we can align ourselves with His will by making choices that promote wellness and longevity. By taking care of our bodies and souls, we can experience the satisfaction of a life well-lived.

What choices can you make in your daily life to promote longevity and wellness? How can you align yourself with God's desire for you to live a long and healthy life?

_____

....

_____

....

_____

....

_____

Prayer Request   **Prayer Granted**

AFFIRMATION
I am grateful for the gift of a long and healthy life, and I commit to making choices that promote wellness and align with God's desire for me.

PRAYER
Dear God, I pray for the gift of a long and healthy life. Help me to make choices that promote wellness and align myself with your will.

Contemplation

1 Peter 2:24

"He himself bore our sins" in His body on the tree, so that we might die to sins and live for righteousness; "by His wounds you have been healed."

Redemption and Healing

Through the wounds of Christ, we have been healed and made whole. By aligning ourselves with His righteousness and grace, we can experience the healing power of His love in our bodies and souls.

How can you align yourself with Christ's healing power in your daily life? What practices can you incorporate into your routine to nurture your connection with Him?

Prayer Request	Prayer Granted

AFFIRMATION
I am healed and restored by the power of Christ. I trust in God's loving
care for my body, mind, and spirit.

PRAYER
*Dear God, thank you for sending your Son to bear my sins and heal my body.
I trust in your power to restore me to complete health and wholeness.*

Contemplation

Psalm 107:19-20

Then they cried to the Lord in their trouble, and He saved them from their distress. He sent out His word and healed them; He rescued them from the grave.

Divine Rescue

When we are in distress, it can be easy to feel helpless and alone. But by turning to the Lord and trusting in His healing power, we can find comfort and strength. Prayer has been shown to have a powerful impact on physical and emotional health, and we can use it to connect with the divine energy within us and bring healing to our bodies and minds.

How can you deepen your prayer practice and invite more healing energy into your life?

_____

....

_____

....

_____

....

Prayer Request　　　**Prayer Granted**

AFFIRMATION
I am open to the healing power of prayer and trust in God's ability to heal me.

PRAYER
*Dear God, thank you for your healing power. I trust in your divine energy
to bring healing to my body, mind, and spirit.*

Contemplation

Isaiah 40:31

But those who hope in the Lord will renew their strength. They will soar on wings like eagles; they will run and not grow weary, they will walk and not be faint.

Empowered by Hope

When we feel weak or tired, it can be tempting to give up and lose hope. But when we place our hope in the Lord, we can tap into a source of strength that will sustain us through even the toughest times. By trusting in God's plan for our lives and believing in His goodness, we can find the energy and motivation we need to keep going.

What can you do to cultivate a sense of hope and trust in your life?

_____

....

_____

....

_____

....

_____

Prayer Request   **Prayer Granted**

AFFIRMATION
I place my hope in the Lord and trust in His ability to renew my strength.

PRAYER
*Dear God, thank you for renewing my strength and giving me hope.
I trust in your plan for my life and believe in your goodness.*

Contemplation

James 5:16

Therefore confess your sins to each other and pray for each other so that you may be healed. The prayer of a righteous person is powerful and effective.

Confess, Pray, Heal

It can be difficult to admit our mistakes and weaknesses, but by confessing our shortcomings to God and to others. When we pray for each other, we tap into the power of collective energy and the healing power of God. Through confession and prayer, we can free ourselves from guilt and shame and experience greater emotional and physical health.

Is there something you need to confess or ask forgiveness for? How can you pray for others and invite the power of God's healing into your life?

_____

....

_____

....

_____

....

_____

Prayer Request   **Prayer Granted**

AFFIRMATION
I am open to the healing power of confession and prayer, and I trust in God's ability to heal me.

PRAYER
Dear God, thank you for the power of confession and prayer.
I trust in your ability to heal me and those around me.

Contemplation

Proverbs 3:7-8

Do not be wise in your own eyes; fear the Lord and shun evil. This will bring health to your body and nourishment to your bones.

Wisdom of Humility

Pride and self-sufficiency can prevent us from receiving the healing we need. Humility and a reverence for God bring health to our bodies and nourishment to our bones.

In what areas of your life do you need to let go of pride and embrace humility in order to experience greater health?

_____

....

_____

....

_____

....

_____

Prayer Request   **Prayer Granted**

....
....
....
....

AFFIRMATION

Through humility and reverence for God, I am experiencing greater health and strength in my body and bones.

PRAYER

Dear God, I surrender my pride and self-sufficiency to you. I trust in your wisdom and provision for my health and well-being.

Contemplation

Jeremiah 33:6

Nevertheless, I will bring health and healing to it; I will heal my people and will let them enjoy abundant peace and security.

Healing Balm of Peace

God desires for us to experience abundance in all areas of our lives, including our health. It's important to trust in God's power to heal and find peace and security in His promises.

How can you trust in God's power to heal and find peace and security in His promises? What steps can you take to align your heart and mind with God's will for your health?

_____

....

_____

....

_____

....

_____

Prayer Request   **Prayer Granted**

AFFIRMATION

I trust in God's power to heal and find peace and security in His promises.

PRAYER

Dear God, thank you for your promises of healing and abundance. Help me to trust in your power and find peace and security in your promises for my health.

Contemplation

Matthew 11:28

Come to me, all you who are weary and burdened, and I will give you rest.

Rest for the Weary

Our bodies need rest in order to function properly and heal. It's important to prioritize rest and relaxation in our lives, both physically and emotionally.

How can you prioritize rest and relaxation in your life? What steps can you take to reduce stress and anxiety?

_____

....

_____

....

_____

....

_____

Prayer Request   **Prayer Granted**

AFFIRMATION
I choose to prioritize rest and relaxation in my life for the sake of my health and well-being.

PRAYER
Dear God, thank you for the rest and relaxation that you provide. Help me to prioritize rest and reduce stress and anxiety in my life.

Contemplation

Psalm 28:7

The Lord is my strength and my shield; in Him my heart trusts, and I am helped; my heart exults, and with my song I give thanks to Him. [ESV]

Shield in the Lord

Trusting in the Lord can give us the strength we need to face life's challenges. When we put our trust in Him, we can find the courage to persevere through difficult times and know that He is with us every step of the way.

In what areas of your life do you struggle to trust in God? How can you work to build your trust in Him and find strength in His presence?

_____

....

_____

....

_____

....

Prayer Request   **Prayer Granted**

AFFIRMATION
I trust in the Lord to provide the strength I need to overcome any obstacle.

PRAYER
*Dear God, I thank you for being my strength and shield. Help me to trust
in you and find the courage to face life's challenges with confidence.*

Contemplation

Revelation 21:4

He will wipe away every tear from their eyes, and death shall be no more, neither shall there be mourning, nor crying, nor pain anymore, for the former things have passed away. [ESV]

Rejoice in God's Promise

The Lord promises to wipe away every tear and make all things new. We can hold onto this promise and have faith in the healing power of God. It's important to let go of negative emotions and beliefs that hold us back from experiencing the fullness of God's healing power.

What negative emotions or beliefs are hindering your ability to experience healing? How can you let go of these and open yourself up to God's healing power?

_____

....

_____

....

_____

....

_____

Prayer Request   **Prayer Granted**

AFFIRMATION
I choose to trust in God's promise of healing and let go of
negative emotions and beliefs.

PRAYER
*Dear God, I thank you for your promise of healing. Help me to let go of
negative emotions and beliefs and trust in your healing power.*

Contemplation

Philippians 4:6

Do not be anxious about anything, but in every situation, by prayer and petition, with thanksgiving, present your requests to God.

Peaceful Prayerful Petition

Anxiety can take a toll on our physical and mental health. Turn our worries over to God through prayer and thanksgiving. By cultivating a spirit of gratitude, we can shift our focus away from our fears and worries and towards the blessings in our lives.

What are some of the worries or anxieties that you are currently carrying? How can you turn to prayer and gratitude to release these worries and trust in God's provision?

_____

....

_____

....

_____

....

_____

Prayer Request   **Prayer Granted**

AFFIRMATION
I choose to release my anxieties and trust in God's provision for my life.

PRAYER
Dear God, I thank you for your provision and ask for your help in releasing my worries and anxieties. Help me to cultivate a spirit of gratitude and trust in your guidance.

Contemplation

Psalm 73:26

My flesh and my heart may fail, but God is the strength of my heart and my portion forever.

Portion of Everlasting

Our physical bodies may fail us and our hearts may feel weak, but we can always turn to God for strength. He is our refuge and our rock, providing us with the strength we need to face any challenge that comes our way.

In what areas of your life do you feel like you need more strength? How can you turn to God to find the inner strength you need to face those challenges?

Prayer Request	Prayer Granted

AFFIRMATION
I trust in God to provide me with the strength I need to face any challenge.

PRAYER
Dear God, thank you for being the strength of my heart. Help me to trust in you when I feel weak and to find the strength I need to face any challenge.

Contemplation

Romans 12:12

Rejoice in hope, be patient in tribulation, be constant in prayer. [ESV]

Rejoice, Persevere

When we face challenging times, it's easy to become discouraged and lose hope. But God calls us to find strength in adversity by staying grounded in our faith and being constant in prayer. We can also find comfort in the hope that God has a plan for us, and that all things work together for good for those who love Him.

**How can you maintain your hope and faith during difficult times?
How can you make prayer a constant part of your daily routine?**

Prayer Request   **Prayer Granted**

AFFIRMATION
I choose to stay grounded in my faith and find strength in challenging times.

PRAYER
Dear God, help me to remain patient and hopeful in times of tribulation.
May prayer be a constant source of strength and comfort for me.

Contemplation

Isaiah 40:29

He gives power to the faint, and to Him who has no might He increases strength. [ESV]

Power for the Faint

Our faith in God can give us the strength we need to overcome physical and emotional challenges. Even when we feel weak, God can give us the power to face our struggles and come out stronger.

How has your faith helped you to overcome challenges in the past? How can you rely on God's strength to face current struggles?

_____

. . . .

_____

. . . .

_____

. . . .

_____

Prayer Request   **Prayer Granted**

AFFIRMATION
I trust in God's power to give me strength and overcome my challenges.

PRAYER
Dear God, I pray for your strength and guidance as I face challenges in my life. Help me to rely on your power and find strength in my faith.

Contemplation

Psalm 147:6

The Lord lifts up the humble; he casts the wicked to the ground. [ESV]

Humility of Healing

Humility is an important part of healing, both physically and spiritually. When we are humble, we are open to receiving help and guidance from others, and we are more receptive to the healing power of God. It's important to acknowledge our weaknesses and limitations and trust in God's guidance and provision.

How can you cultivate humility in your life to help with your healing journey? How can you trust in God's guidance and provision for your healing?

_____

....

_____

....

_____

....

Prayer Request   **Prayer Granted**

AFFIRMATION

I choose to cultivate humility and trust in God's guidance and provision for my healing journey.

PRAYER

Dear God, help me to cultivate humility and trust in your guidance and provision for my healing. May I be open to receiving help and guidance from others as I journey towards wellness.

Contemplation

Psalm 55:22

Cast your cares on the Lord and he will sustain you; he will never let the righteous be shaken.

Trusting in the Sustainer

It's natural to have worries and concerns in life, but we don't have to carry the weight of them alone. God is always there to sustain us and lift us up. When we trust in Him and give our worries to Him, we can find peace and rest.

What are some worries or concerns that you have been carrying on your own? How can you begin to cast them on the Lord and trust in His sustaining power?

_____

....

_____

....

_____

....

Prayer Request   **Prayer Granted**

....

....

....

....

AFFIRMATION
I choose to trust in God's sustaining power and cast my cares on Him.

PRAYER
Dear God, thank you for sustaining me and lifting me up. Help me to trust in you and cast my cares on you.

Contemplation

Psalm 121:1-2

I lift up my eyes to the mountains—where does my help come from? My help comes from the Lord, the Maker of heaven and earth.

Looking Up

When we are faced with challenges and difficulties, it's easy to get bogged down in our worries and concerns. But when we look up to God and ask for His help, we can receive the guidance and strength we need to persevere. It's important to remember that our help comes from the Maker of heaven and earth, who has infinite wisdom and power.

In what areas of your life do you need to look up for help? How can you cultivate a habit of seeking God's guidance and strength?

_____

....

_____

....

_____

....

Prayer Request	Prayer Granted
....	....
....	....
....	....
....	....

AFFIRMATION
I choose to look up to God for help and guidance in all areas of my life.

PRAYER
Dear God, thank you for being the Maker of heaven and earth and the source of my help. Help me to look up to you for guidance and strength.

Contemplation

Psalm 18:2

The Lord is my rock, my fortress and my deliverer; my God is my rock, in whom I take refuge, my shield and the horn of my salvation, my stronghold.

Refuge in God

When we are feeling overwhelmed or under attack, remember to know God as our rock, fortress, and deliverer. He is a strong and unchanging presence that we can take refuge in. It's important to remember that God is always there for us and will never abandon us.

In what areas of your life do you feel vulnerable and in need of God's strength? How can you turn to Him and find refuge in His love?

_____

....

_____

....

_____

....

Prayer Request　　　　**Prayer Granted**

AFFIRMATION
I find strength in God and His love surrounds me, protecting me from harm.

PRAYER
Dear God, thank you for being my rock and my fortress. Help me to find strength in you and take refuge in your love and protection.

Contemplation

Isaiah 54:17

No weapon formed against you shall prosper, and every tongue which rises against you in judgment you shall condemn. This is the heritage of the servants of the Lord, and their righteousness is from me," says the Lord. [NKJV]

Divine Protection

God promises to protect us from harm and defend us against those who speak ill of us. It's important to trust in God's protection and know that no weapon formed against us shall prosper. Focus inward for the source of truth and never outward at circumstances, and experiences.

How can you trust in God's protection and release your fears of harm or judgment? What specific actions or words can you use to remind yourself of God's divine protection?

_____

....

_____

....

_____

....

Prayer Request   **Prayer Granted**

AFFIRMATION

I trust in God's divine protection and know that no weapon formed
against me shall prosper.

PRAYER

*Dear God, thank you for your divine protection. Help me to trust in your
protection and release my fears of harm or judgment.*

Contemplation

John 10:10

The thief comes only to steal and kill and destroy; I came that they may have life, and have it abundantly. [RSV]

Abundant Is Life

Jesus came to give us an abundant life, full of joy, love, and peace. It's important to remember that we deserve to live an abundant life and that God wants us to enjoy the blessings He has given us.

In what areas of your life do you feel lack? How can you invite abundance into those areas and trust that God desires abundance for you?

_____

....

_____

....

_____

....

Prayer Request   **Prayer Granted**

AFFIRMATION
I deserve to live an abundant life and trust in God's blessings.

PRAYER
Dear God, thank you for the abundant life you have given me. Help me to see the abundance in my life and trust in your blessings.

Contemplation

Ephesians 2:10

For we are God's handiwork, created in Christ Jesus to do good works, which God prepared in advance for us to do.

Purposeful Creation

As we face pain and suffering, it can be hard to see the purpose behind it all. But we are reminded that we are God's masterpiece. Every masterpiece can go through a few rough drafts. Focus on the good work you are here to do through it all.

What is your understanding of your purpose in Christ? How can you seek out and fulfill the good works God has prepared in advance for you to do?

_____

....

_____

....

_____

....

Prayer Request   **Prayer Granted**

AFFIRMATION

I am created in Christ to fulfill a unique purpose and impact the world for good.

PRAYER

Dear God, thank you for creating me with a unique purpose. Help me to seek out and fulfill the good works you have prepared in advance for me to do.

Contemplation

Matthew 5:23-24

Therefore if you are offering your gift at the altar and there remember that your brother or sister has something against you, leave your gift there in front of the altar. First go and be reconciled to them; then come and offer your gift.

Peace before Presentations

Jesus teaches us the importance of reconciling with others before coming to offer our gifts at the altar. It's important to seek out reconciliation and forgiveness with others, not only for our spiritual well-being but for the well-being of our relationships and communities.

In what relationships or situations do you need to seek out reconciliation and forgiveness? How can you take steps towards reconciliation with others?

_____

....

_____

....

_____

....

Prayer Request   **Prayer Granted**

AFFIRMATION
I choose to let go of anger and practice forgiveness for the sake of my health and well-being.

PRAYER
Dear God, I ask for the strength to practice forgiveness and seek reconciliation in my relationships. Help me to let go of anger and negative emotions for the sake of my health and well-being.

Contemplation

John 13:34

A new command I give you: Love one another. As I have loved you, so you must love one another.

Love One Another

Love is not just an emotion, it is an action. It is the selfless giving of oneself for the benefit of another. Practicing love can have a positive impact on our physical and emotional health, as well as the health of our relationships with others.

How can you show love to someone today, even in a small way?
How can you cultivate a habit of selfless love towards others?

_____

....

_____

....

_____

....

Prayer Request   **Prayer Granted**

AFFIRMATION

I choose to show love to others, as a means of improving my own health and the health of my relationships.

PRAYER

Dear God, thank you for the healing power of love. Help me to cultivate a habit of selfless love towards others, as a means of improving my own health and the health of my relationships.

Contemplation

Psalm 107:9

For he satisfies the thirsty and fills the hungry with good things.

God's Provision

God promises to provide for our needs abundantly. It's important to trust in his provision and seek out the good things that he has in store for us.

What good things has God provided for you in your life? How can you seek out and appreciate the abundance of God's provision in your life?

_____

....

_____

....

_____

....

_____

Prayer Request	Prayer Granted
....	....
....	....
....	....
....	....

AFFIRMATION
I trust in God's abundance and know that all my needs will be met.

PRAYER
Dear God, thank you for providing abundantly for my needs. Help me to trust in your provision and seek out the good things that you have in store for me.

Contemplation

Psalm 23:6

Surely your goodness and love will follow me all the days of my life, and I will dwell in the house of the Lord forever.

Love Follows Always

God's goodness and love are restorative and renewing, and can bring healing to our hearts and minds. By focusing on God's goodness, we can find peace and restoration.

How can you focus on God's goodness in your life, even in difficult circumstances? How can you find peace and restoration in His love?

_____

....

_____

....

_____

....

_____

Prayer Request

....

....

....

....

Prayer Granted

....

....

....

....

AFFIRMATION
I choose to focus on God's goodness and find peace and restoration in His love.

PRAYER
Dear God, thank you for your goodness and love, which are restorative and renewing. Help me to focus on your goodness and find peace and restoration in your love.

Contemplation

Psalm 34:18

The Lord is close to the brokenhearted and saves those who are crushed in spirit.

Savior of the Crushed

When we're feeling brokenhearted or crushed in spirit, it can be easy to feel alone and isolated. But this verse assures us that the Lord is close to us in these times and will save us. It's important to turn to the Lord for comfort and strength.

In what ways do you turn to the Lord for comfort during difficult times? How can you strengthen your relationship with Him and trust in His comfort?

_____

....

_____

....

_____

....

_____

Prayer Request	Prayer Granted
....	....
....	....
....	....
....	....

AFFIRMATION
I find comfort in the Lord during difficult times and trust in His strength.

PRAYER
Dear God, thank you for being close to me during difficult times.
Help me to trust in your comfort and strength when I'm feeling
brokenhearted or crushed in spirit.

Contemplation

Romans 8:28

And we know that in all things God works for the good of those who love Him, who have been called according to his purpose.

God's Goodness

When we're going through difficult times, it can be hard to see the good in it. But this verse assures us that God works all things for the good of those who love Him. It's important to trust in His plan and purpose for our lives.

In what ways have you seen God work things for good in your life, even in difficult times? How can you strengthen your faith and trust in His plan?

_____

....

_____

....

_____

....

Prayer Request   **Prayer Granted**

AFFIRMATION

I trust in God's plan for my life, because of Him, I can weather through any storm.

PRAYER

Dear God, thank you for working all things for good in my life. Help me to trust in your plan and purpose, even in difficult times.

Contemplation

Philippians 4:19

And my God will meet all your needs according to the riches of his glory in Christ Jesus.

Richness For All

Sometimes in times of hardship we focus heavily on what we lack. But God promises to bless us abundantly in all things at all times. So it's important to focus on what we want to increase and turn our minds away from what we want to decrease.

In what areas of your life are you holding onto worry about your needs? How can you affirm your trust in God's abundance and let go of worry?

_____

....

_____

....

_____

....

_____

Prayer Request   **Prayer Granted**

AFFIRMATION
I commit to releasing worry and doubt knowing that I am wonderfully made in God's image.

PRAYER
Dear God, thank you for meeting all my needs. Help me to trust in your provision and let go of worry.

Contemplation

Proverbs 4:23

Above all else, guard your heart, for everything you do flows from it.

Focused Heart

Our thoughts and emotions can have a profound impact on our overall well-being. It's important to be mindful of what we allow into our hearts and minds, and to guard against undeserving thoughts and emotions that can drain our energy and diminish our health.

What negative thoughts or emotions do you struggle with? How can you guard your heart against them and cultivate positive thoughts and emotions instead?

_____

....

_____

....

_____

....

Prayer Request   **Prayer Granted**

....

....

....

....

AFFIRMATION
I choose to guard my heart against negativity and cultivate positive thoughts and emotions for the sake of my health and well-being.

PRAYER
Dear God, I ask for your help in guarding my heart and mind against negativity. Help me to cultivate positive thoughts and emotions for my health and well-being.

Contemplation

John 8:36

So if the Son sets you free, you will be free indeed.

Freedom of Healing

True healing is not just a physical process, but a spiritual one as well. When we allow ourselves to be open to the healing power of God, we can experience a sense of freedom and liberation from the burdens that weigh us down.

What burdens do you need to release in order to experience healing and freedom? How can you open yourself up to the healing power of God?

_____

....

_____

....

_____

....

Prayer Request   **Prayer Granted**

....

....

....

....

AFFIRMATION
I choose to lay down my burdens and allow God's healing power to set me free.

PRAYER
Dear God, I ask for your healing power to set me free from the burdens that weigh me down. Help me to release what no longer serves me and embrace the freedom of healing.

Contemplation

Psalm 23:2-3

He makes me lie down in green pastures, he leads me beside quiet waters, he refreshes my soul. He guides me along the right paths for his name's sake.

Rest and Refreshment

In order to maintain good health, it's important to prioritize rest and refreshment for our bodies and minds. God leads us to places of rest and refreshment, and it's up to us to take the time to be still and receive the nourishment our souls need.

Are you over burdened or taking on too much, which is causing stress? What activities or practices help you feel rested and nourished?

_____

....

_____

....

_____

....

Prayer Request   **Prayer Granted**

AFFIRMATION
I prioritize rest and refreshment for the sake of my physical, emotional, and spiritual health.

PRAYER
Dear God, I thank you for leading me to places of rest and refreshment. Help me to prioritize rest and take the time to nourish my body, mind, and soul.

Contemplation

John 14:27

Peace I leave with you; my peace I give you. I do not give to you as the world gives. Do not let your hearts be troubled and do not be afraid.

Peaceful Heart

In a world filled with stress and anxiety, it can be difficult to find a sense of peace. But Jesus promises to give us his peace, which is unlike anything the world can offer. It's up to us to receive this gift and allow it to calm our troubled hearts.

What areas of your life are overcommitted and boggled down? How can you invite Jesus' peace into those areas and allow it to calm your troubled heart?

_____

....

_____

....

_____

....

_____

Prayer Request	Prayer Granted

AFFIRMATION
I receive the gift of Jesus' peace and allow it to calm my troubled heart.

PRAYER
Dear God, thank you for the gift of Jesus' peace. Help me to receive it and allow it to calm my troubled heart.

Contemplation

Philippians 4:7

And the peace of God, which transcends all understanding, will guard your hearts and your minds in Christ Jesus.

The Peace of God

God promises us a peace that is beyond understanding, a peace that can guard our hearts and minds in even the most difficult of circumstances. Cultivate a relationship with Him and allow His peace to flood you life.

Are you truly giving yourself over to the power of God? How can you cultivate a deeper relationship with God and learn to accept in His peace in all situations?

_____

....

_____

....

_____

....

_____

Prayer Request   **Prayer Granted**

AFFIRMATION
I choose to trust in the peace of God, and let it flood my life.

PRAYER
Dear God, thank you for the peace that transcends all understanding. Help me to cultivate a deeper relationship with you and bask in your peace.

Contemplation

Colossians 2:6-7

So then, just as you received Christ Jesus as Lord, continue to live your lives in Him, rooted and built up in him, strengthened in the faith as you were taught, and overflowing with thankfulness.

Rooted and Built Up

Just as a tree needs roots to remain firmly planted and strong, we must remain rooted in Christ to live a life of strength and stability. By strengthening our faith and living in gratitude, we can be built up in Christ and experience the abundance of His blessings.

In what ways can you deepen your roots in Christ? How can you cultivate gratitude in your daily life to strengthen your faith?

Prayer Request   **Prayer Granted**

AFFIRMATION

I am rooted and built up in Christ, strengthened by faith and overflowing with thankfulness.

PRAYER

Dear God, thank you for the blessings of being rooted and built up in Christ. Help me to deepen my faith and cultivate gratitude in my daily life.

Contemplation

2 Corinthians 5:17

Therefore, if anyone is in Christ, the new creation has come: The old has gone, the new is here!

Renewed Creation

In Christ, we have the opportunity to become a new creation, shedding our old selves and stepping into a new life filled with purpose and hope. It's important to embrace this new identity and allow God to transform us from the inside out.

In what areas of your life do you feel stuck in your old self? How can you embrace your new identity in Christ and allow God to transform you?

_____

....

_____

....

_____

....

_____

Prayer Request   **Prayer Granted**

AFFIRMATION

I am a new creation in Christ, and I choose to embrace this new identity and allow God to transform me from the inside out.

PRAYER

Dear God, thank you for making me a new creation in Christ. Help me to fully embrace this new identity and allow you to transform me from the inside out.

Contemplation

John 5:8-9

Then Jesus said to him, 'Get up! Pick up your mat and walk.' At once the man was cured; he picked up his mat and walked.

Guided To Heal

The story of the man who was cured by Jesus shows us the power of faith and action. When we believe and take action towards our goals, we can experience the healing power of God in our lives. It's important to have faith and take action towards our goals, even when the path may seem difficult.

**What actions can you take towards your health and healing goals?
How can you strengthen your faith to believe in the power of
God's healing in your life?**

....

....

....

....

....

....

Prayer Request	Prayer Granted

AFFIRMATION
I have faith in the power of God to heal me and I take action towards
my health and healing goals.

PRAYER
*Dear God, thank you for the healing power of faith and action. Help me to
believe in your healing power and take action towards my
health and healing goals.*

Thank you for your purchase! Please leave us a review by going to:

go.azizituere.com/healingreview

It helps us to continue to strive for excellence to bring you great content.

...and don't forget to check out these great journals as well!

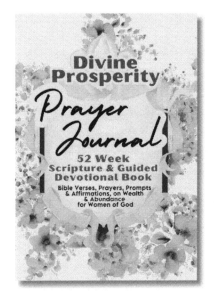

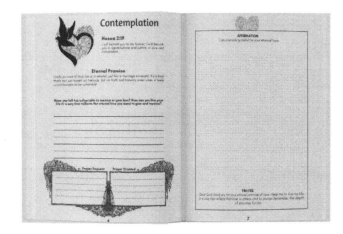

Made in the USA
Columbia, SC
27 December 2024

50717409R00061